THIS HIKING JOURNAL

names: _____

address: _____

phone: _____

email: _____

IN CASE OF EMERGENCY PLEASE CONTACT:

name: _____

address: _____

phone: _____

email: _____

OUR HIKES

#	TRAIL / HIKE	LOCATION	DISTANCE	DURATION
1				
2				
3				
4				
5				
6				
7				
8				
9				
10				
11				
12				
13				
14				
15				
16				
17				
18				
19				
20				
21				
22				
23				
24				
25				

OUR HIKES

#	TRAIL / HIKE	LOCATION	DISTANCE	DURATION
26				
27				
28				
29				
30				
31				
32				
33				
34				
35				
36				
37				
38				
39				
40				
41				
42				
43				
44				
45				
46				
47				
48				
49				
50				

HIKE #1

Trail		Date	
Location		We hiked with	
Starting Point			

Start Time	End Time
Distance	Duration
Elevation Gain	Elevation Loss

Difficulty Level ☆☆☆☆☆
Endurance ☆☆☆☆☆
Scenery ☆☆☆☆☆
Trail Traffic ☆☆☆☆☆
Romance ♡♡♡♡♡
Overall Rating ☆☆☆☆☆

Weather Conditions

Terrain / Trail Conditions

Facilities / Refreshment / Water Supply

Stages

Starting Point	(Intermediate) Destination	Distance	Height	Time

What we liked most

Notes

Nature observed

Height (feet)

Distance (miles) / Time (hours)

When finished, we felt

HIKE #2

Trail
Location
Starting Point

Date
We hiked with

Start Time	End Time
Distance	Duration
Elevation Gain	Elevation Loss

Difficulty Level ☆☆☆☆☆
Endurance ☆☆☆☆☆
Scenery ☆☆☆☆☆
Trail Traffic ☆☆☆☆☆
Romance ♡♡♡♡♡
Overall Rating ☆☆☆☆☆

Weather Conditions

Terrain / Trail Conditions

Facilities / Refreshment / Water Supply

Stages				
Starting Point	(Intermediate) Destination	Distance	Height	Time

| What we liked most |

| Notes |

| Nature observed | Height (feet)

Distance (miles) / Time (hours) |

| When finished, we felt |

HIKE #3

Trail
Location
Starting Point

Date
We hiked with

Start Time	End Time
Distance	Duration
Elevation Gain	Elevation Loss

Difficulty Level ☆☆☆☆☆
Endurance ☆☆☆☆☆
Scenery ☆☆☆☆☆
Trail Traffic ☆☆☆☆☆
Romance ♡♡♡♡♡
Overall Rating ☆☆☆☆☆

Weather Conditions

Terrain / Trail Conditions

Facilities / Refreshment / Water Supply

Stages				
Starting Point	(Intermediate) Destination	Distance	Height	Time

What we liked most

Notes

Nature observed

Height (feet)

Distance (miles) / Time (hours)

When finished, we felt

HIKE #4

Trail

Location

Starting Point

Start Time	End Time
Distance	Duration
Elevation Gain	Elevation Loss

Date

We hiked with

Difficulty Level ☆☆☆☆☆
Endurance ☆☆☆☆☆
Scenery ☆☆☆☆☆
Trail Traffic ☆☆☆☆☆
Romance ♡♡♡♡♡
Overall Rating ☆☆☆☆☆

Weather Conditions

Terrain / Trail Conditions

Facilities / Refreshment / Water Supply

Stages

Starting Point	(Intermediate) Destination	Distance	Height	Time

What we liked most

Notes

Nature observed

Height (feet)

Distance (miles) / Time (hours)

When finished, we felt

HIKE #5

Trail		Date
Location		We hiked with
Starting Point		

Start Time	End Time
Distance	Duration
Elevation Gain	Elevation Loss

Difficulty Level ☆☆☆☆☆
Endurance ☆☆☆☆☆
Scenery ☆☆☆☆☆
Trail Traffic ☆☆☆☆☆
Romance ♡♡♡♡♡
Overall Rating ☆☆☆☆☆

Weather Conditions

Terrain / Trail Conditions

Facilities / Refreshment / Water Supply

Stages

Starting Point	(Intermediate) Destination	Distance	Height	Time

What we liked most

Notes

Nature observed	Height (feet)
	Distance (miles) / Time (hours)

When finished, we felt

HIKE #6

Trail	Date
Location	We hiked with
Starting Point	

Start Time	End Time
Distance	Duration
Elevation Gain	Elevation Loss

Difficulty Level ☆☆☆☆☆
Endurance ☆☆☆☆☆
Scenery ☆☆☆☆☆
Trail Traffic ☆☆☆☆☆
Romance ♡♡♡♡♡
Overall Rating ☆☆☆☆☆

Weather Conditions

Terrain / Trail Conditions

Facilities / Refreshment / Water Supply

Stages				
Starting Point	(Intermediate) Destination	Distance	Height	Time

What we liked most

Notes

Nature observed

Height (feet)

Distance (miles) / Time (hours)

When finished, we felt

HIKE #7

Trail
Location
Starting Point

Date
We hiked with

Start Time	End Time
Distance	Duration
Elevation Gain	Elevation Loss

Difficulty Level ☆☆☆☆☆
Endurance ☆☆☆☆☆
Scenery ☆☆☆☆☆
Trail Traffic ☆☆☆☆☆
Romance ♡♡♡♡♡
Overall Rating ☆☆☆☆☆

Weather Conditions

Terrain / Trail Conditions

Facilities / Refreshment / Water Supply

Stages				
Starting Point	(Intermediate) Destination	Distance	Height	Time

What we liked most

Notes

Nature observed

Height (feet)

Distance (miles) / Time (hours)

When finished, we felt

HIKE #8

Trail
Location
Starting Point

Start Time	End Time
Distance	Duration
Elevation Gain	Elevation Loss

Date
We hiked with

Difficulty Level ☆☆☆☆☆
Endurance ☆☆☆☆☆
Scenery ☆☆☆☆☆
Trail Traffic ☆☆☆☆☆
Romance ♡♡♡♡♡
Overall Rating ☆☆☆☆☆

Weather Conditions

Terrain / Trail Conditions

Facilities / Refreshment / Water Supply

Stages				
Starting Point	(Intermediate) Destination	Distance	Height	Time

What we liked most

Notes

Nature observed

Height (feet)

Distance (miles) / Time (hours)

When finished, we felt

HIKE #9

Trail

Location

Starting Point

Start Time	End Time
Distance	Duration
Elevation Gain	Elevation Loss

Date

We hiked with

Difficulty Level ☆☆☆☆☆
Endurance ☆☆☆☆☆
Scenery ☆☆☆☆☆
Trail Traffic ☆☆☆☆☆
Romance ♡♡♡♡♡
Overall Rating ☆☆☆☆☆

Weather Conditions

Terrain / Trail Conditions

Facilities / Refreshment / Water Supply

Stages

Starting Point	(Intermediate) Destination	Distance	Height	Time

What we liked most

Notes

Nature observed

Height (feet)

Distance (miles) / Time (hours)

When finished, we felt

HIKE #10

Trail		Date	
Location		We hiked with	
Starting Point			

Start Time	End Time
Distance	Duration
Elevation Gain	Elevation Loss

Difficulty Level ☆☆☆☆☆
Endurance ☆☆☆☆☆
Scenery ☆☆☆☆☆
Trail Traffic ☆☆☆☆☆
Romance ♡♡♡♡♡
Overall Rating ☆☆☆☆☆

Weather Conditions

Terrain / Trail Conditions

Facilities / Refreshment / Water Supply

Stages				
Starting Point	(Intermediate) Destination	Distance	Height	Time

What we liked most

Notes

Nature observed

Height (feet)

Distance (miles) / Time (hours)

When finished, we felt

HIKE #11

Trail	Date
Location	We hiked with
Starting Point	

Start Time	End Time
Distance	Duration
Elevation Gain	Elevation Loss

Difficulty Level ☆☆☆☆☆
Endurance ☆☆☆☆☆
Scenery ☆☆☆☆☆
Trail Traffic ☆☆☆☆☆
Romance ♡♡♡♡♡
Overall Rating ☆☆☆☆☆

Weather Conditions

Terrain / Trail Conditions

Facilities / Refreshment / Water Supply

Stages				
Starting Point	(Intermediate) Destination	Distance	Height	Time

What we liked most

Notes

Nature observed

Height (feet)

Distance (miles) / Time (hours)

When finished, we felt

HIKE #12

Trail	Date
Location	We hiked with
Starting Point	

Start Time	End Time
Distance	Duration
Elevation Gain	Elevation Loss

Difficulty Level ☆☆☆☆☆
Endurance ☆☆☆☆☆
Scenery ☆☆☆☆☆
Trail Traffic ☆☆☆☆☆
Romance ♡♡♡♡♡
Overall Rating ☆☆☆☆☆

Weather Conditions

Terrain / Trail Conditions

Facilities / Refreshment / Water Supply

Stages				
Starting Point	(Intermediate) Destination	Distance	Height	Time

What we liked most

Notes

Nature observed	Height (feet)
	Distance (miles) / Time (hours)

When finished, we felt

HIKE #13

Trail
Location
Starting Point

Start Time	End Time
Distance	Duration
Elevation Gain	Elevation Loss

Date
We hiked with

Difficulty Level ☆☆☆☆☆
Endurance ☆☆☆☆☆
Scenery ☆☆☆☆☆
Trail Traffic ☆☆☆☆☆
Romance ♡♡♡♡♡
Overall Rating ☆☆☆☆☆

Weather Conditions

Terrain / Trail Conditions

Facilities / Refreshment / Water Supply

Stages				
Starting Point	(Intermediate) Destination	Distance	Height	Time

What we liked most

Notes

Nature observed

Height (feet)

Distance (miles) / Time (hours)

When finished, we felt

HIKE #14

Trail
Location
Starting Point

Start Time	End Time
Distance	Duration
Elevation Gain	Elevation Loss

Date
We hiked with

Difficulty Level ☆☆☆☆☆
Endurance ☆☆☆☆☆
Scenery ☆☆☆☆☆
Trail Traffic ☆☆☆☆☆
Romance ♡♡♡♡♡
Overall Rating ☆☆☆☆☆

Weather Conditions

Terrain / Trail Conditions

Facilities / Refreshment / Water Supply

Stages				
Starting Point	(Intermediate) Destination	Distance	Height	Time

What we liked most

Notes

Nature observed

Height (feet)

Distance (miles) / Time (hours)

When finished, we felt

HIKE #15

Trail
Location
Starting Point

Date
We hiked with

Start Time	End Time
Distance	Duration
Elevation Gain	Elevation Loss

Difficulty Level ☆☆☆☆☆
Endurance ☆☆☆☆☆
Scenery ☆☆☆☆☆
Trail Traffic ☆☆☆☆☆
Romance ♡♡♡♡♡
Overall Rating ☆☆☆☆☆

Weather Conditions

Terrain / Trail Conditions

Facilities / Refreshment / Water Supply

Stages

Starting Point	(Intermediate) Destination	Distance	Height	Time

What we liked most

Notes

Nature observed	Height (feet)
	Distance (miles) / Time (hours)

When finished, we felt

HIKE #16

Trail

Location

Starting Point

Start Time	End Time

Distance	Duration

Elevation Gain	Elevation Loss

Date

We hiked with

Difficulty Level ☆☆☆☆☆
Endurance ☆☆☆☆☆
Scenery ☆☆☆☆☆
Trail Traffic ☆☆☆☆☆
Romance ♡♡♡♡♡
Overall Rating ☆☆☆☆☆

Weather Conditions

Terrain / Trail Conditions

Facilities / Refreshment / Water Supply

Stages				
Starting Point	(Intermediate) Destination	Distance	Height	Time

What we liked most

Notes

Nature observed

Height (feet)

Distance (miles) / Time (hours)

When finished, we felt

HIKE #17

Trail		Date
Location		We hiked with
Starting Point		

		Difficulty Level	☆☆☆☆☆
Start Time	End Time	Endurance	☆☆☆☆☆
		Scenery	☆☆☆☆☆
Distance	Duration	Trail Traffic	☆☆☆☆☆
		Romance	♡♡♡♡♡
Elevation Gain	Elevation Loss	**Overall Rating**	☆☆☆☆☆

Weather Conditions

Terrain / Trail Conditions

Facilities / Refreshment / Water Supply

Stages

Starting Point	(Intermediate) Destination	Distance	Height	Time

What we liked most

Notes

Nature observed	Height (feet)
	Distance (miles) / Time (hours)

When finished, we felt

HIKE #18

Trail
Location
Starting Point

Start Time	End Time
Distance	Duration
Elevation Gain	Elevation Loss

Date
We hiked with

Difficulty Level ☆☆☆☆☆
Endurance ☆☆☆☆☆
Scenery ☆☆☆☆☆
Trail Traffic ☆☆☆☆☆
Romance ♡♡♡♡♡
Overall Rating ☆☆☆☆☆

Weather Conditions

Terrain / Trail Conditions

Facilities / Refreshment / Water Supply

Stages				
Starting Point	(Intermediate) Destination	Distance	Height	Time

What we liked most

Notes

Nature observed

Height (feet)

Distance (miles) / Time (hours)

When finished, we felt

HIKE #19

Trail

Location

Starting Point

Date

We hiked with

Start Time	End Time
Distance	Duration
Elevation Gain	Elevation Loss

Difficulty Level ☆☆☆☆☆
Endurance ☆☆☆☆☆
Scenery ☆☆☆☆☆
Trail Traffic ☆☆☆☆☆
Romance ♡♡♡♡♡
Overall Rating ☆☆☆☆☆

Weather Conditions

Terrain / Trail Conditions

Facilities / Refreshment / Water Supply

Stages				
Starting Point	(Intermediate) Destination	Distance	Height	Time

What we liked most

Notes

Nature observed

Height (feet)

Distance (miles) / Time (hours)

When finished, we felt

HIKE #20

Trail		Date	
Location		We hiked with	
Starting Point			

Start Time	End Time
Distance	Duration
Elevation Gain	Elevation Loss

Difficulty Level ☆☆☆☆☆
Endurance ☆☆☆☆☆
Scenery ☆☆☆☆☆
Trail Traffic ☆☆☆☆☆
Romance ♡♡♡♡♡
Overall Rating ☆☆☆☆☆

Weather Conditions

Terrain / Trail Conditions

Facilities / Refreshment / Water Supply

Stages				
Starting Point	(Intermediate) Destination	Distance	Height	Time

| What we liked most |

| Notes |

| Nature observed | Height (feet)

Distance (miles) / Time (hours) |

| When finished, we felt |

HIKE #21

Trail
Location
Starting Point

Start Time	End Time
Distance	Duration
Elevation Gain	Elevation Loss

Date
We hiked with

Difficulty Level ☆☆☆☆☆
Endurance ☆☆☆☆☆
Scenery ☆☆☆☆☆
Trail Traffic ☆☆☆☆☆
Romance ♡♡♡♡♡
Overall Rating ☆☆☆☆☆

Weather Conditions

Terrain / Trail Conditions

Facilities / Refreshment / Water Supply

Stages				
Starting Point	(Intermediate) Destination	Distance	Height	Time

What we liked most

Notes

Nature observed

Height (feet)

Distance (miles) / Time (hours)

When finished, we felt

HIKE #22

Trail
Location
Starting Point

Date
We hiked with

Start Time	End Time
Distance	Duration
Elevation Gain	Elevation Loss

Difficulty Level ☆☆☆☆☆
Endurance ☆☆☆☆☆
Scenery ☆☆☆☆☆
Trail Traffic ☆☆☆☆☆
Romance ♡♡♡♡♡
Overall Rating ☆☆☆☆☆

Weather Conditions

Terrain / Trail Conditions

Facilities / Refreshment / Water Supply

Stages

Starting Point	(Intermediate) Destination	Distance	Height	Time

What we liked most

Notes

Nature observed

Height (feet)

Distance (miles) / Time (hours)

When finished, we felt

HIKE #23

Trail
Location
Starting Point

Start Time	End Time
Distance	Duration
Elevation Gain	Elevation Loss

Date
We hiked with

Difficulty Level ☆☆☆☆☆
Endurance ☆☆☆☆☆
Scenery ☆☆☆☆☆
Trail Traffic ☆☆☆☆☆
Romance ♡♡♡♡♡
Overall Rating ☆☆☆☆☆

Weather Conditions

Terrain / Trail Conditions

Facilities / Refreshment / Water Supply

Stages				
Starting Point	(Intermediate) Destination	Distance	Height	Time

What we liked most

Notes

Nature observed	Height (feet)
	Distance (miles) / Time (hours)

When finished, we felt

HIKE #24

Trail
Location
Starting Point

Date
We hiked with

Start Time	End Time
Distance	Duration
Elevation Gain	Elevation Loss

Difficulty Level ☆☆☆☆☆
Endurance ☆☆☆☆☆
Scenery ☆☆☆☆☆
Trail Traffic ☆☆☆☆☆
Romance ♡♡♡♡♡
Overall Rating ☆☆☆☆☆

Weather Conditions

Terrain / Trail Conditions

Facilities / Refreshment / Water Supply

Stages				
Starting Point	(Intermediate) Destination	Distance	Height	Time

What we liked most

Notes

Nature observed	Height (feet)
	Distance (miles) / Time (hours)

When finished, we felt

HIKE #25

Trail		Date	
Location		We hiked with	
Starting Point			

Start Time	End Time
Distance	Duration
Elevation Gain	Elevation Loss

Difficulty Level ☆☆☆☆☆
Endurance ☆☆☆☆☆
Scenery ☆☆☆☆☆
Trail Traffic ☆☆☆☆☆
Romance ♡♡♡♡♡
Overall Rating ☆☆☆☆☆

Weather Conditions

Terrain / Trail Conditions

Facilities / Refreshment / Water Supply

Stages				
Starting Point	(Intermediate) Destination	Distance	Height	Time

What we liked most

Notes

Nature observed

Height (feet)

Distance (miles) / Time (hours)

When finished, we felt

HIKE #26

Trail	Date
Location	We hiked with
Starting Point	

Start Time	End Time
Distance	Duration
Elevation Gain	Elevation Loss

Difficulty Level ☆☆☆☆☆
Endurance ☆☆☆☆☆
Scenery ☆☆☆☆☆
Trail Traffic ☆☆☆☆☆
Romance ♡♡♡♡♡
Overall Rating ☆☆☆☆☆

Weather Conditions

Terrain / Trail Conditions

Facilities / Refreshment / Water Supply

Stages				
Starting Point	(Intermediate) Destination	Distance	Height	Time

What we liked most

Notes

Nature observed

Height (feet)

Distance (miles) / Time (hours)

When finished, we felt

HIKE #27

Trail	Date
Location	We hiked with
Starting Point	

Start Time	End Time
Distance	Duration
Elevation Gain	Elevation Loss

Difficulty Level ☆☆☆☆☆
Endurance ☆☆☆☆☆
Scenery ☆☆☆☆☆
Trail Traffic ☆☆☆☆☆
Romance ♡♡♡♡♡
Overall Rating ☆☆☆☆☆

Weather Conditions

Terrain / Trail Conditions

Facilities / Refreshment / Water Supply

Stages

Starting Point	(Intermediate) Destination	Distance	Height	Time

What we liked most

Notes

Nature observed

Height (feet)

Distance (miles) / Time (hours)

When finished, we felt

HIKE #28

Trail
Location
Starting Point

Date
We hiked with

Start Time	End Time
Distance	Duration
Elevation Gain	Elevation Loss

Difficulty Level ☆☆☆☆☆
Endurance ☆☆☆☆☆
Scenery ☆☆☆☆☆
Trail Traffic ☆☆☆☆☆
Romance ♡♡♡♡♡
Overall Rating ☆☆☆☆☆

Weather Conditions

Terrain / Trail Conditions

Facilities / Refreshment / Water Supply

Stages				
Starting Point	(Intermediate) Destination	Distance	Height	Time

What we liked most

Notes

Nature observed

Height (feet)

Distance (miles) / Time (hours)

When finished, we felt

HIKE #29

Trail
Location
Starting Point

Date
We hiked with

Start Time	End Time
Distance	Duration
Elevation Gain	Elevation Loss

Difficulty Level ☆☆☆☆☆
Endurance ☆☆☆☆☆
Scenery ☆☆☆☆☆
Trail Traffic ☆☆☆☆☆
Romance ♡♡♡♡♡
Overall Rating ☆☆☆☆☆

Weather Conditions

Terrain / Trail Conditions

Facilities / Refreshment / Water Supply

Stages

Starting Point	(Intermediate) Destination	Distance	Height	Time

What we liked most

Notes

Nature observed

Height (feet)

Distance (miles) / Time (hours)

When finished, we felt

HIKE #30

Trail		Date	
Location		We hiked with	
Starting Point			

Start Time	End Time
Distance	Duration
Elevation Gain	Elevation Loss

Difficulty Level ☆☆☆☆☆
Endurance ☆☆☆☆☆
Scenery ☆☆☆☆☆
Trail Traffic ☆☆☆☆☆
Romance ♡♡♡♡♡
Overall Rating ☆☆☆☆☆

Weather Conditions

Terrain / Trail Conditions

Facilities / Refreshment / Water Supply

Stages

Starting Point	(Intermediate) Destination	Distance	Height	Time

What we liked most

Notes

Nature observed

Height (feet)

Distance (miles) / Time (hours)

When finished, we felt

HIKE #31

Trail
Location
Starting Point

Date
We hiked with

Start Time	End Time
Distance	Duration
Elevation Gain	Elevation Loss

Difficulty Level ☆☆☆☆☆
Endurance ☆☆☆☆☆
Scenery ☆☆☆☆☆
Trail Traffic ☆☆☆☆☆
Romance ♡♡♡♡♡
Overall Rating ☆☆☆☆☆

Weather Conditions

Terrain / Trail Conditions

Facilities / Refreshment / Water Supply

Stages				
Starting Point	(Intermediate) Destination	Distance	Height	Time

What we liked most

Notes

Nature observed

Height (feet)

Distance (miles) / Time (hours)

When finished, we felt

HIKE #32

Trail	Date
Location	We hiked with
Starting Point	

Start Time	End Time
Distance	Duration
Elevation Gain	Elevation Loss

Difficulty Level ☆☆☆☆☆
Endurance ☆☆☆☆☆
Scenery ☆☆☆☆☆
Trail Traffic ☆☆☆☆☆
Romance ♡♡♡♡♡
Overall Rating ☆☆☆☆☆

Weather Conditions

Terrain / Trail Conditions

Facilities / Refreshment / Water Supply

Stages

Starting Point	(Intermediate) Destination	Distance	Height	Time

| What we liked most |

| Notes |

| Nature observed | Height (feet) vs Distance (miles) / Time (hours) |

| When finished, we felt |

HIKE #33

Trail

Location

Starting Point

Start Time	End Time
Distance	Duration
Elevation Gain	Elevation Loss

Date

We hiked with

Difficulty Level ☆☆☆☆☆
Endurance ☆☆☆☆☆
Scenery ☆☆☆☆☆
Trail Traffic ☆☆☆☆☆
Romance ♡♡♡♡♡
Overall Rating ☆☆☆☆☆

Weather Conditions

Terrain / Trail Conditions

Facilities / Refreshment / Water Supply

Stages

Starting Point	(Intermediate) Destination	Distance	Height	Time

What we liked most

Notes

Nature observed

Height (feet)

Distance (miles) / Time (hours)

When finished, we felt

HIKE #34

Trail
Location
Starting Point

Date
We hiked with

Start Time	End Time
Distance	Duration
Elevation Gain	Elevation Loss

Difficulty Level ☆☆☆☆☆
Endurance ☆☆☆☆☆
Scenery ☆☆☆☆☆
Trail Traffic ☆☆☆☆☆
Romance ♡♡♡♡♡
Overall Rating ☆☆☆☆☆

Weather Conditions

Terrain / Trail Conditions

Facilities / Refreshment / Water Supply

Stages				
Starting Point	(Intermediate) Destination	Distance	Height	Time

What we liked most

Notes

Nature observed	Height (feet)
	Distance (miles) / Time (hours)

When finished, we felt

HIKE #35

Trail
Location
Starting Point

Date
We hiked with

Difficulty Level ☆☆☆☆☆
Endurance ☆☆☆☆☆
Scenery ☆☆☆☆☆
Trail Traffic ☆☆☆☆☆
Romance ♡♡♡♡♡
Overall Rating ☆☆☆☆☆

Start Time	End Time
Distance	Duration
Elevation Gain	Elevation Loss

Weather Conditions

Terrain / Trail Conditions

Facilities / Refreshment / Water Supply

Stages				
Starting Point	(Intermediate) Destination	Distance	Height	Time

What we liked most

Notes

Nature observed	Height (feet)
	Distance (miles) / Time (hours)

When finished, we felt

HIKE #36

Trail
Location
Starting Point

Date
We hiked with

Start Time	End Time
Distance	Duration
Elevation Gain	Elevation Loss

Difficulty Level ☆☆☆☆☆
Endurance ☆☆☆☆☆
Scenery ☆☆☆☆☆
Trail Traffic ☆☆☆☆☆
Romance ♡♡♡♡♡
Overall Rating ☆☆☆☆☆

Weather Conditions

Terrain / Trail Conditions

Facilities / Refreshment / Water Supply

Stages

Starting Point	(Intermediate) Destination	Distance	Height	Time

| What we liked most |

| Notes |

| Nature observed | Height (feet) |
| | Distance (miles) / Time (hours) |

| When finished, we felt |

HIKE #37

Trail		Date	
Location		We hiked with	
Starting Point			

Start Time	End Time
Distance	Duration
Elevation Gain	Elevation Loss

Difficulty Level ☆☆☆☆☆
Endurance ☆☆☆☆☆
Scenery ☆☆☆☆☆
Trail Traffic ☆☆☆☆☆
Romance ♡♡♡♡♡
Overall Rating ☆☆☆☆☆

Weather Conditions

Terrain / Trail Conditions

Facilities / Refreshment / Water Supply

Stages				
Starting Point	(Intermediate) Destination	Distance	Height	Time

What we liked most

Notes

Nature observed

Height (feet)

Distance (miles) / Time (hours)

When finished, we felt

HIKE #38

Trail
Location
Starting Point

Date
We hiked with

Start Time	End Time
Distance	Duration
Elevation Gain	Elevation Loss

Difficulty Level ☆☆☆☆☆
Endurance ☆☆☆☆☆
Scenery ☆☆☆☆☆
Trail Traffic ☆☆☆☆☆
Romance ♡♡♡♡♡
Overall Rating ☆☆☆☆☆

Weather Conditions

Terrain / Trail Conditions

Facilities / Refreshment / Water Supply

Stages				
Starting Point	(Intermediate) Destination	Distance	Height	Time

What we liked most

Notes

Nature observed

Height (feet)

Distance (miles) / Time (hours)

When finished, we felt

HIKE #39

Trail

Location

Starting Point

Start Time	End Time
Distance	Duration
Elevation Gain	Elevation Loss

Date

We hiked with

Difficulty Level ☆☆☆☆☆
Endurance ☆☆☆☆☆
Scenery ☆☆☆☆☆
Trail Traffic ☆☆☆☆☆
Romance ♡♡♡♡♡
Overall Rating ☆☆☆☆☆

Weather Conditions

Terrain / Trail Conditions

Facilities / Refreshment / Water Supply

Stages				
Starting Point	(Intermediate) Destination	Distance	Height	Time

What we liked most

Notes

Nature observed

Height (feet)

Distance (miles) / Time (hours)

When finished, we felt

HIKE #40

Trail	Date
Location	We hiked with
Starting Point	

Start Time	End Time
Distance	Duration
Elevation Gain	Elevation Loss

Difficulty Level ☆☆☆☆☆
Endurance ☆☆☆☆☆
Scenery ☆☆☆☆☆
Trail Traffic ☆☆☆☆☆
Romance ♡♡♡♡♡
Overall Rating ☆☆☆☆☆

Weather Conditions

Terrain / Trail Conditions

Facilities / Refreshment / Water Supply

Stages				
Starting Point	(Intermediate) Destination	Distance	Height	Time

What we liked most

Notes

Nature observed

Height (feet)

Distance (miles) / Time (hours)

When finished, we felt

HIKE #41

Trail		Date	
Location		We hiked with	
Starting Point			

Start Time	End Time
Distance	Duration
Elevation Gain	Elevation Loss

Difficulty Level ☆☆☆☆☆
Endurance ☆☆☆☆☆
Scenery ☆☆☆☆☆
Trail Traffic ☆☆☆☆☆
Romance ♡♡♡♡♡
Overall Rating ☆☆☆☆☆

Weather Conditions

Terrain / Trail Conditions

Facilities / Refreshment / Water Supply

Stages

Starting Point	(Intermediate) Destination	Distance	Height	Time

What we liked most

Notes

| Nature observed | Height (feet)

Distance (miles) / Time (hours) |
| --- | --- |

When finished, we felt

HIKE #42

Trail

Location

Starting Point

Start Time	End Time
Distance	Duration
Elevation Gain	Elevation Loss

Date

We hiked with

Difficulty Level ☆☆☆☆☆
Endurance ☆☆☆☆☆
Scenery ☆☆☆☆☆
Trail Traffic ☆☆☆☆☆
Romance ♡♡♡♡♡
Overall Rating ☆☆☆☆☆

Weather Conditions

Terrain / Trail Conditions

Facilities / Refreshment / Water Supply

Stages				
Starting Point	(Intermediate) Destination	Distance	Height	Time

| What we liked most |

| Notes |

| Nature observed | Height (feet) |
| | Distance (miles) / Time (hours) |

| When finished, we felt |

HIKE #43

Trail		Date	
Location		We hiked with	
Starting Point			

Start Time	End Time
Distance	Duration
Elevation Gain	Elevation Loss

Difficulty Level ☆☆☆☆☆
Endurance ☆☆☆☆☆
Scenery ☆☆☆☆☆
Trail Traffic ☆☆☆☆☆
Romance ♡♡♡♡♡
Overall Rating ☆☆☆☆☆

Weather Conditions

Terrain / Trail Conditions

Facilities / Refreshment / Water Supply

Stages				
Starting Point	(Intermediate) Destination	Distance	Height	Time

What we liked most

Notes

Nature observed

Height (feet)

Distance (miles) / Time (hours)

When finished, we felt

HIKE #44

Trail	Date
Location	We hiked with
Starting Point	

Start Time	End Time
Distance	Duration
Elevation Gain	Elevation Loss

Difficulty Level ☆☆☆☆☆
Endurance ☆☆☆☆☆
Scenery ☆☆☆☆☆
Trail Traffic ☆☆☆☆☆
Romance ♡♡♡♡♡
Overall Rating ☆☆☆☆☆

Weather Conditions

Terrain / Trail Conditions

Facilities / Refreshment / Water Supply

Stages				
Starting Point	(Intermediate) Destination	Distance	Height	Time

What we liked most

Notes

Nature observed

Height (feet)

Distance (miles) / Time (hours)

When finished, we felt

HIKE #45

Trail
Location
Starting Point

Start Time	End Time
Distance	Duration
Elevation Gain	Elevation Loss

Date
We hiked with

Difficulty Level ☆☆☆☆☆
Endurance ☆☆☆☆☆
Scenery ☆☆☆☆☆
Trail Traffic ☆☆☆☆☆
Romance ♡♡♡♡♡
Overall Rating ☆☆☆☆☆

Weather Conditions

Terrain / Trail Conditions

Facilities / Refreshment / Water Supply

Stages				
Starting Point	(Intermediate) Destination	Distance	Height	Time

What we liked most

Notes

Nature observed	Height (feet)
	Distance (miles) / Time (hours)

When finished, we felt

HIKE #46

Trail	Date
Location	We hiked with
Starting Point	

Start Time	End Time
Distance	Duration
Elevation Gain	Elevation Loss

Difficulty Level ☆☆☆☆☆
Endurance ☆☆☆☆☆
Scenery ☆☆☆☆☆
Trail Traffic ☆☆☆☆☆
Romance ♡♡♡♡♡
Overall Rating ☆☆☆☆☆

Weather Conditions

Terrain / Trail Conditions

Facilities / Refreshment / Water Supply

Stages

Starting Point	(Intermediate) Destination	Distance	Height	Time

What we liked most

Notes

Nature observed

Height (feet)

Distance (miles) / Time (hours)

When finished, we felt

HIKE #47

Trail		Date	
Location		We hiked with	
Starting Point			

Start Time	End Time
Distance	Duration
Elevation Gain	Elevation Loss

Difficulty Level ☆☆☆☆☆
Endurance ☆☆☆☆☆
Scenery ☆☆☆☆☆
Trail Traffic ☆☆☆☆☆
Romance ♡♡♡♡♡
Overall Rating ☆☆☆☆☆

Weather Conditions

Terrain / Trail Conditions

Facilities / Refreshment / Water Supply

Stages				
Starting Point	(Intermediate) Destination	Distance	Height	Time

| What we liked most |

| Notes |

| Nature observed | Height (feet)

Distance (miles) / Time (hours) |

| When finished, we felt |

HIKE #48

Trail
Location
Starting Point

Date
We hiked with

Start Time	End Time
Distance	Duration
Elevation Gain	Elevation Loss

Difficulty Level ☆☆☆☆☆
Endurance ☆☆☆☆☆
Scenery ☆☆☆☆☆
Trail Traffic ☆☆☆☆☆
Romance ♡♡♡♡♡
Overall Rating ☆☆☆☆☆

Weather Conditions

Terrain / Trail Conditions

Facilities / Refreshment / Water Supply

Stages				
Starting Point	(Intermediate) Destination	Distance	Height	Time

What we liked most

Notes

Nature observed

Height (feet)

Distance (miles) / Time (hours)

When finished, we felt

HIKE #49

Trail
Location
Starting Point

Start Time	End Time
Distance	Duration
Elevation Gain	Elevation Loss

Date
We hiked with

Difficulty Level ☆☆☆☆☆
Endurance ☆☆☆☆☆
Scenery ☆☆☆☆☆
Trail Traffic ☆☆☆☆☆
Romance ♡♡♡♡♡
Overall Rating ☆☆☆☆☆

Weather Conditions

Terrain / Trail Conditions

Facilities / Refreshment / Water Supply

Stages				
Starting Point	(Intermediate) Destination	Distance	Height	Time

What we liked most

Notes

Nature observed

Height (feet)

Distance (miles) / Time (hours)

When finished, we felt

HIKE #50

Trail

Location

Starting Point

Start Time	End Time
Distance	Duration
Elevation Gain	Elevation Loss

Date

We hiked with

Difficulty Level ☆☆☆☆☆
Endurance ☆☆☆☆☆
Scenery ☆☆☆☆☆
Trail Traffic ☆☆☆☆☆
Romance ♡♡♡♡♡
Overall Rating ☆☆☆☆☆

Weather Conditions

Terrain / Trail Conditions

Facilities / Refreshment / Water Supply

Stages				
Starting Point	(Intermediate) Destination	Distance	Height	Time

What we liked most

Notes

Nature observed

Height (feet)

Distance (miles) / Time (hours)

When finished, we felt

© 2019 LIDDELBOOKS
SIMON ZIEGER
OSTERSEENSTR. 34
82393 IFFELDORF
GERMANY

QUESTIONS OR SUGGESTIONS?
LIDDELBOOKS@GMX.DE

HAVE FUN WITH YOUR LIDDELBOOK!

Made in the USA
Monee, IL
20 November 2024